Wiltshire

Nigel Vile

COUNTRYSIDE BOOKS
NEWBURY BERKSHIRE

First Published 2006
© Nigel Vile, 2006

COUNTRYSIDE BOOKS
3 Catherine Road
Newbury, Berkshire

To view our complete range of books,
please visit us at
www.countrysidebooks.co.uk

ISBN 1 85306 967 1
EAN 978 1 85306 967 3

Cover picture of Castle Combe
supplied by Bill Meadows

Photographs by the author
Designed by Peter Davies, Nautilus Design
Produced through MRM Associates Ltd, Reading
Printed by Woolnough Bookbinding Ltd., Irthlingborough

Contents

Location map   4

Introduction   5

POCKET PUB WALKS

1	Cricklade (5 miles)	7
2	Sherston (6 miles)	12
3	Castle Combe (6 miles)	17
4	Heddington (3 miles)	22
5	Avebury (3½ miles)	27
6	Aldbourne (8 miles)	32
7	Bradford-on-Avon (3½ miles)	37
8	Bratton (4 miles)	42
9	Wilton (3½ miles)	47
10	Heytesbury (6 miles)	52
11	Horningsham (4 miles)	57
12	Stourton (6 miles)	61
13	Stonehenge & Shrewton (4 miles)	66
14	Donhead St Andrew (4 miles)	71
15	Tollard Royal (6 miles)	77

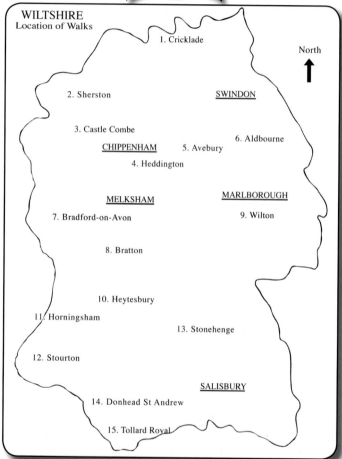

WILTSHIRE
Location of Walks

1. Cricklade

North ↑

2. Sherston

SWINDON

3. Castle Combe

CHIPPENHAM   5. Avebury   6. Aldbourne

4. Heddington

MELKSHAM   MARLBOROUGH

7. Bradford-on-Avon   9. Wilton

8. Bratton

10. Heytesbury

11. Horningsham

13. Stonehenge

12. Stourton

SALISBURY

14. Donhead St Andrew

15. Tollard Royal

Introduction

What better way to spend a leisurely few hours than to combine a walk with a visit to a traditional pub for a delicious meal or snack and a glass of beer or wine? The routes in this book allow you to do just that. Each circuit – which all include a recommended pub or are just a short drive to one – takes you through some of the finest scenery in Wiltshire, one of the best-loved counties in England from a walker's perspective.

There is the well-known chalk downland, rising to almost 1,000 feet above sea level at Tan Hill, east of Devizes. Below the chalk hills lie the clay vales, rich dairying and arable pastures that border rivers like the Wylye, the Kennet and the Avon. Many of Britain's most famous prehistoric remains are here: vast stone circles at Stonehenge and Avebury; West Kennett with its famed long barrow; above Bratton and Westbury a white horse gleaming on the chalk hillside.

There are also the stunning villages and towns, all carved from the glorious local bedrock – Castle Combe, for example, as well as Bradford-on-Avon. Add the great landed estates at Longleat and Stourhead, as well as the upper reaches of the Thames at Cricklade and the glorious hanging valleys on Cranborne Chase at Tollard Royal, and you have as delightful a series of landscape types as you could wish to experience and enjoy.

These 15 circular walks are between 3 and 8 miles in length. Car parking options have been suggested in the vicinity of each pub, although in many cases it will be possible to park at the hostelry itself. In such cases, you must of course be a customer and be sure to seek the landlord's permission before leaving your car while you are walking. A sketch map, indicating the route to be followed, accompanies each walk.

To make your day complete, don't forget to carry a snack and a drink in that trustworthy rucksack, as well as a decent set of waterproofs. Despite occasional belief to the contrary, the authors of walking guidebooks cannot guarantee their readers sunny weather!

It just remains for me to wish you many happy hours of pleasure in following these pub walks.

I can be contacted through my website. If you have comments on any of these walks, please email me and any necessary amendments will be posted up in order to help other readers and users of this book. The website address is: www.geocities.com/vilewalks/nigel

Nigel Vile

Publisher's Note

We hope that you obtain considerable enjoyment from this book; great care has been taken in its preparation. However, changes of landlord and actual closures are sadly not uncommon. Likewise, although at the time of publication all routes followed public rights of way or permitted paths, diversion orders can be made and permissions withdrawn.

We cannot, of course, be held responsible for such diversion orders and any inaccuracies in the text which result from these or any other changes to the routes nor any damage which might result from walkers trespassing on private property. We are anxious though that all details covering the walks and pubs are kept up to date and would therefore welcome information from readers which would be relevant to future editions.

The simple sketch maps that accompany the walks in this book are based on notes made by the author whilst checking out the routes on the ground. However, for the benefit of a proper map, we do recommend that you purchase the relevant Ordnance Survey sheet covering your walk. The Ordnance Survey maps are widely available, especially through booksellers and local newsagents.

The Red Lion Inn

Cricklade has a rich archaeological heritage, including fortified Saxon town walls and two contrasting churches in St Sampson's and St Mary's. The main street is lined with many 17th- and 18th-century buildings, as well as being the location of the market cross. The town lies alongside the infant River Thames, whose banks are followed on this walk across North Meadow, an old flower-rich hay meadow, towards journey's end. This watery theme continues with tantalising glimpses of the Cotswold Water Park – a series of flooded former gravel workings – as well as a stretch of the long defunct Thames & Severn Canal. With water, water, everywhere, this is not a walk to be tackled following periods of heavy rainfall!

Distance – 5 miles.

OS Explorer 169 Cirencester and Swindon. GR 100934.

A flat landscape – be prepared for some muddy patches.

Starting point The free car park by the town hall at the Swindon end of Cricklade's High Street.

How to get there Cricklade lies just off of the A419 Cirencester road, 7 miles north-west of Swindon.

THE PUB

The **Red Lion** is a friendly, award-winning 16th-century ale house at the north end of Cricklade's High Street, near the end of the walk. Indeed, recently it served its 1,000th different beer! The hostelry features up to eight ever-changing guest ales from local and micro-brewers and, until recently, survived on the strength of its drink sales alone. Traditional pub food is now served in the back bar, however, with the Sunday carvery being particularly recommended. With its old-fashioned hospitality and warm welcome, the Red Lion is a pub not to be missed if you are a lover of real ales and proper pubs.

Opening times: 12 noon to 11 pm on Monday to Saturday, 10.30 pm on Sundays. No food available on Mondays.
☎ *01793 750776*

1 Leave the car park, turn right and walk along Cricklade's **High Street** as far the **Kings Head pub**. Turn left into **Church Lane**, enter the churchyard and bear right to join the road running alongside the church. Follow this road to the left, past the fire station, and on for 350 yards to a road junction. Turn right, then first left into **Stones Lane**. Follow this lane to the next junction,

turn right past the sports centre and continue for just over ¾ mile to the gateposts at the entrance to **Hailstone House**. Keep ahead and, where the driveway bears right to the house, continue ahead along a green lane and drop downhill for 250 yards to a footbridge over the **Thames**. Continue along the track beyond the river for 250 yards to a junction and, ignoring the left turn, follow the track ahead – it shortly bears right – for 250 yards to a junction with a broad track.

2 Turn left, and follow this track for ½ mile through to a lane. Turn right along this lane and, on a right-hand bend in 300 yards, pass through the metal handgate ahead, before following the right edge of the field ahead to a gate and small paddock in the far corner of the field. Beyond this paddock, join a lane in **Cerney Wick**, turn left and, at the next junction in just 25 yards, keep on the main lane that bears right. In 100 yards, immediately past the **Crown Inn**, turn right and follow the lane ahead for 150 yards to reach the bed of the **Thames & Severn**

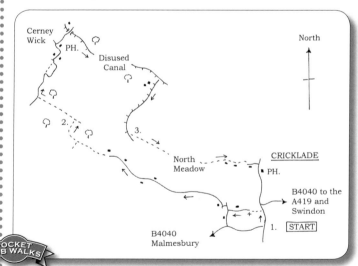

The Cotswold Water Park.

Canal. Follow the towpath to the right for ¾ mile to a gate and drive just beyond the remains of its junction with the **North Wiltshire Canal**. Follow the drive to the right and, where it enters the grounds of a property, keep ahead on an enclosed path that shortly bears right to join the towpath of the former North Wiltshire Canal. Follow the path to the left for 500 yards to a footbridge over the **River Thames**, 100 yards beyond a bridge over a smaller stream.

3 Do not cross the Thames – instead cross a stile on the left to enter **North Meadow**. Follow the Thames across this meadow to a handgate, before continuing across two meadows beside the river heading back to **Cricklade**. In approximately 546 yards, cross a footbridge over the river and walk up past a barn to

a handgate. Just past this gate, turn left and follow the **Thames Path** – an enclosed path at this point – to a gate and paddock. Bear half right to a gate and an area of new housing. Follow the path to the left and, where the pavement bears right, cross an area of grass to a gap in the trees ahead and an open field. Follow the Thames Path

This handsome property in Cricklade dates from 1708.

across this large field, and a smaller field beyond, to reach a lane. Turn left along to the junction of this lane with Cricklade's **High Street**, turn right and continue back to the car park.

Places of interest nearby

The **Swindon & Cricklade Railway** is Wiltshire's only standard-gauge Heritage Railway. It is based on the site of Blunsdon Station between Swindon and Cirencester, and visitors can enjoy all the facilities they expect from a Heritage Railway centre, including regular steam services each Sunday. The line is a section of the Midland & South Western Junction Railway, a minor railway of just under 60 route miles. While its passenger services ran between Southampton and Cheltenham, its own metals began at Red Post Junction outside Andover and ended at Andoversford. The towns along the line included Marlborough, Swindon, Cricklade and Cirencester.

☎ *01793 771615 (weekends only) for more information on the Swindon & Cricklade Railway; website: www.swindon-cricklade-railway.org*

The Rattlebone Inn

Sherston lies on the south-eastern fringes of the **Cotswolds,** amidst a landscape that owes more to its native Wiltshire surroundings than the limestone of the wolds. Whilst the walk passes through countryside that is pleasant, if unspectacular, the various attractions along the route make this a worthwhile excursion. Sherston itself, with its wide High Street and ancient church, is worth an hour of anybody's time. Then there is the village of Easton Grey, which is pure Cotswold in character and feel. This stone settlement is centred upon a five-arched bridge that spans the Avon, overlooked by the distant Easton Grey House and church. Between these two fine villages, our steps cross a landscape watered by the upper reaches of the Bristol Avon. Quiet byways and little-walked tracks convey a certain remoteness – very much far from the madding crowd.

Distance – 6 miles.

OS Explorer 168 Stroud, Tetbury and Malmesbury. GR 853858.

A gently undulating landscape.

Starting point Sherston's wide main street just to the west of the Rattlebone Inn.

How to get there Sherston lies on the B4040 midway between Acton Turville and Malmesbury. Park in the wide High Street where there is ample roadside parking.

THE PUB Named after John Rattlebone, a local knight who fought bravely against King Canute in 1016, the **Rattlebone Inn** dates back to the 17th century. With its whitewashed exterior – and its Cotswold stone roof – this fine old hostelry has a most welcoming appearance. As well as offering fare that ranges from light snacks to meals that would grace a restaurant, fine beers from both Young's and Smiles breweries are available. If the name does sound vaguely familiar, yes this was the pub that made national headlines for being one of Prince Harry's locals!

Opening times: 12 noon to 11 pm on Monday to Saturday, 10.30 pm on Sundays.
☎ *01666 840871*

1 Walk along the **High Street**, and follow the B4040 to the right of the village shop, past the **Rattlebone Inn** and **Sherston church** and continue for 400 yards to a crossroads. Turn left into **Tetbury Road** and walk ahead for 400 yards to reach **Vancelettes Farm**, the last residence in Sherston. Continue

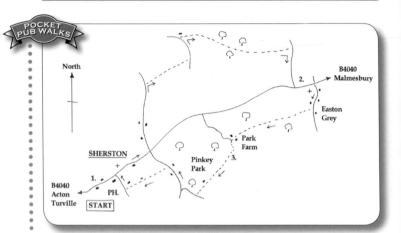

along **Tetbury Road** for a further 500 yards to a pair of metal gates on the right-hand side. Pass through this gateway – there is no footpath sign – and head across an open arable field to a gap in the far-right corner. Pass through this gap and follow the right edges of the following two fields to reach a quiet lane. Turn left and, on a left-hand bend in 500 yards, turn right along a waymarked bridleway alongside some agricultural sheds. Follow what is initially an enclosed track for 250 yards into an open field. Continue along this track as it runs along the left edges of three fields before entering woodland in ½ mile. Continue along the track for another ½ mile to reach a quiet lane, turn right and continue for 350 yards to its junction with the B4040.

2 Turn left and, in 200 yards, right at a minor crossroads down into **Easton Grey**. Drop downhill into the village and, having crossed the **River Avon**, continue for 40 yards to a handgate on the right and a footpath. Turn right and follow a track uphill through a belt of trees into an open field. Cross this field, keeping a fence on the right, to a pair of stiles in the far-right corner. Head across to the far-left corner of the next field where a handgate leads into a small enclosure. Walk down the left-hand end of this enclosure

to a stile in the bottom left-hand corner. Follow the right edge of the following field, **Pinkney Mill** and the **Avon** below on the right, to a stile in the corner of the field. Cross the next field to a stile opposite, before following an enclosed path between the buildings of **Park Farm** down to a lane opposite **Scot's Farm**. Turn left, and follow a track uphill from the farm, pass through a gateway ahead at the top of a gentle climb and continue ahead to a wall that borders **Pinkney Park**. Follow the wall around to a gate in 100 yards.

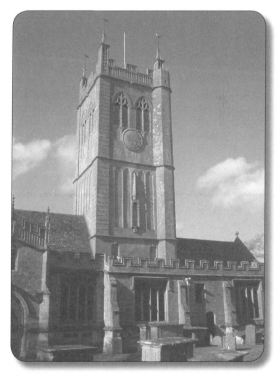

Sherston church.

Wiltshire

3 Beyond this gate, follow the line of a fence on the right ahead and, on the far side of the field, continue for 400 yards along a track, passing cottages on the right, before joining an unclassified road. Turn right and drop downhill to a road junction in 300 yards. Turn right, cross the **Avon** and continue uphill for 150 yards before following a footpath on the left signposted to **Tanners Hill**, opposite the entrance to **Lower Farm**. Enter a paddock and cross to a stile in the wooden fence opposite. Head across to a handgate in the far-right corner of the next paddock. Pass through this gate – ignoring a handgate on the right – and continue along the path ahead that runs between the back gardens of some houses on the right and a field on the left. At the far side of the field, continue down a metalled path to reach a road in a housing estate. Follow the path opposite down to **Tanners Hill**, turn right and continue uphill to **Church Street** in Sherston. A left turn returns the walk to the **High Street**.

Places of interest nearby

Malmesbury, just a few miles north-east of Sherston, claims to be England's oldest borough and has a recorded history that goes back 1,500 years. In its heyday, the famous **Malmesbury Abbey** was one of the largest buildings in the country and, as William of Malmesbury noted in 1143, 'fairer than anything in England'. Alongside the abbey are the **Abbey House Gardens**, with its five acres of colour no matter what the season of the year. The delightful displays slope down to the banks of the River Avon, and have featured on nationwide television programmes such as *Gardener's World*.

☎ *for the gardens: 01666 822212; Malmesbury's Tourist Information Centre: 01666 823748.*

The White Hart

The By Brook is arguably the most attractive of the Bristol Avon's tributaries. Flowing from deep in the Southern Cotswolds, it passes through steep wooded valleys to Castle Combe and Ford, Slaughterford and Box, before joining the Avon at Bathford. The rich array of habitats in the valley – woodland and wetland, water meadows and limestone grassland – are home to an equally rich array of flora and fauna, including buzzards and kestrel, hare and badger, butterfly and orchids. Castle Combe is one of England's most delightful villages, and the view up through the main street from the packhorse bridge that crosses the By Brook has launched any number of calendars and greetings cards, chocolate boxes and biscuit tins! This walk encompasses all of these elements and much more besides. It provides the perfect counter argument to those who believe the Cotswolds only exist north of Cirencester.

THE PUB

The **White Hart** is set in the pretty village of Castle Combe, which was used as the setting for the film *Dr Doolittle* in the mid 1960s and is an extremely popular spot for tourists. The pub has many charming interior features and a beer garden and courtyard at the rear of the building. The menu is extensive and there is an excellent selection of real ales to choose from, with the focus being on Wadworth beers such as 6X and Farmers Glory. With parking in the village being rather difficult – and with the White Hart having no car park – this is one walk where the hostelry appears along the way.

Opening times: 11 am to 3 pm and 6 pm to 11 pm.
☎ *01249 782295*

Distance – 6 miles.

OS Explorer 156 Chippenham and Bradford-on-Avon. GR 845777.

Lanes, tracks and fieldpaths in and around the By Brook valley.

Starting point The visitors' car park in Upper Castle Combe.

How to get there *Upper Castle Combe lies on the B4039 midway between Chippenham and Acton Turville. The car park is clearly signposted from the main road.*

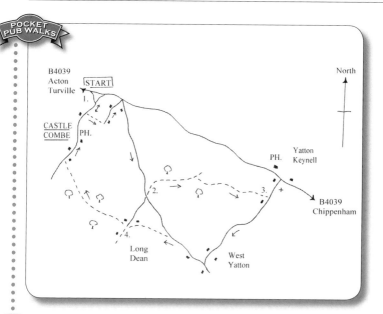

POCKET PUB WALKS

1 Leave the car park, turn right and, at a junction in just 100 yards, turn right to follow the road down into **Castle Combe**. In 250 yards, just past **Castle Combe Museum** and opposite a property called **Hill House**, turn left onto a bridleway. In 300 yards, at the top of a climb, turn left at a junction and follow a back lane to its junction with the B4039 in **Upper Castle Combe**. Turn right down past a bungalow called **Maples**, and follow a level lane alongside the local motor sport race track for ¾ mile, before continuing downhill through woodland for 500 yards to a handgate on the left by a Nature Reserve sign, just before a right turn into **Long Dean**.

2 Pass through this handgate, follow the path to the left – it soon bears right – and walk through a dry limestone valley – the **West Yatton Down Reserve**. On the far side of the valley, pass through a gate and follow a woodland path for 450 yards to a

Castle Combe through which the By Brook flows.

gate and open field. Turn right and follow a field path under electricity wires up to a stile in the end field boundary. Walk directly ahead up through the next field to a wooden fence in the top left corner of the field. Beyond this wooden fence, follow an enclosed path up to a stile by a barn conversion, continue ahead to a gate and proceed along the track up to the lane by **Yatton Keynell Manor**. Detour to the left for 200 yards if you wish to visit **St Margaret's church** in Yatton Keynell.

3 **For the main walk**, turn right past the manor and continue for 1 mile to a junction in **West Yatton** by **Ivy Farm**. Take the right turn to Castle Combe and Long Dean and, in ½ mile, as the lane begins to drop downhill into **Chapel Wood**, fork left along an

unmarked footpath. Drop downhill through the woodland to a junction of paths in **Long Dean** by **Nut Tree Cottage**. Turn right and, at the next junction, follow the path that runs to the left of **Rose Cottage** and the local letterbox.

4 Follow the track ahead uphill out of Long Dean to a gate on the hilltop, before continuing ahead to a second gate just 25 yards ahead. Continue following the hilltop path high above the **By Brook** through woodland until the path emerges onto more open hillside in ½ mile. Keep ahead, following the left-hand field boundary, to a stile in the far-left corner of the field by By Brook. Continue along the path by the river, before crossing a bridge to join the Ford to Castle Combe road. Turn right, and walk into **Castle Combe**, the **White Hart Inn** lying on the right by the **Market Cross** in just 300 yards. Having visited this fine hostelry, follow the road to the right up out of Castle Combe, before turning left in 400 yards to return to the car park.

Places of interest nearby

The nearest town to Castle Combe is **Chippenham**, originally a Saxon market place on the River Avon. The oldest part of the town lies around St Mary's church, where there are a number of 16th- and 17th-century properties. These historic dwellings reflect the town's former days as a cloth centre. The history of Chippenham can be best discovered by visiting the Museum and Heritage Centre in the Market Place.
☎ *01249 705020 for details.*

Castle Combe Museum, with its displays relating to the history of this most attractive village, is passed along the way just above the White Hart. Opening hours are restricted to Sunday afternoons between Easter and October.
☎ *01249 782250 for further information*

The Ivy Inn

The Wiltshire village of Heddington starred in one of the first fly-on-the-wall documentaries when, in the 1970s, life in this quiet settlement featured in a weekly television series called 'The Diary of a Village'. Every argument and dispute at the parish-pump fell under the microscope, and the nation sat entranced. Above the village, on Roundway Down, a more significant dispute took place in 1643 when Sir William Waller was defeated by Royalist forces in a bloody Civil War battle. On the western tip of Roundway Down lies the hillfort of Oliver's Castle, triangular in shape and enclosing a site of some three acres. The expansive views make it easy to see why this hilltop was chosen as the site for this ancient fortification. Close at hand lie Devizes, Melksham and the Avon Vale, while in the distance the Cotswold Hills, the Mendips and points further afield can be picked out.

THE PUB

The **Ivy Inn** is more than 400 years old and is a delightful half-timbered and thatched hostelry. Formerly three separate cottages that have been knocked into one, its inn sign depicts three species of ivy with their Latin botanical names. It is a popular watering hole and its food enjoys an enviable reputation locally. Being part of the Wadworth estate, fine ales such as 6X and IPA are always available.

Opening times: 12 noon to 3 pm and 6.30 pm to 11 pm.
☎ *01380 850276*

Distance – 3 miles.

OS Explorers 156 Chippenham and Bradford-on-Avon and 157 Marlborough and Savernake Forest. GR 999662.

Quiet lanes, tracks and fieldpaths, with one climb onto the North Wessex Downs.

Starting point The roadside by Heddington church, a few minutes' walk from the Ivy Inn.

How to get there From the A4 a mile east of Calne town centre, head south along an unclassified road to Heddington. In 2½ miles, just past the Ivy Inn at Heddington, at the junction with Church Road, turn left and park by the church.

1 Continue along **Church Road**, the church on the right, for 150 yards to a junction with **Hampsley Road** by a small green. Turn right and, in 100 yards, by the barns of **Church Farm**, keep on the lane as it bears left uphill towards the downs. In 600 yards,

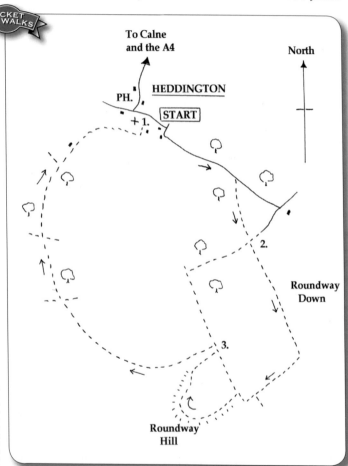

POCKET
PUB WALKS

To Calne
and the A4

North

HEDDINGTON

PH.

START

+1.

2.

Roundway
Down

3.

Roundway
Hill

On Roundway Down.

just past a stile and Nature Reserve on the left, cross a stile on the right into a 'bumpy' hillside field. Follow the right-hand of two gullies ahead uphill and, on reaching the hilltop, walk across to a stile, gate and lane in the far-right corner of the field.

2 Turn right and, in 20 yards, left along a byway. Follow this track across **Roundway Down** and, in 500 yards, keep on the byway as it bears right and continue for 150 yards to a car parking area for Roundway Down. Follow the track to the right out of this parking area – ignoring the gate at the end of the car park – and, in 20 yards, pass through a gate on the left-hand side. Follow the hilltop path ahead out to the end of **Roundway Hill**, with its fine view across West Wiltshire. Bear right on reaching the edge of the hilltop, and walk past a few isolated beech trees before

continuing along the edge of the escarpment to a **Roundway Hill information board**. Beyond this board, keep on the track as it bears right through a gateway to reach a gate in 80 yards and a track on the edge of Roundway Down.

3 On reaching this gate, turn around and follow a track downhill through the escarpment. At the foot of the slope, keep on this track – it bears right – and continue for ½ mile along the foot of the escarpment to reach a cross track coming down off the hillside. Ignore the gateway opposite – instead pass through a gap to the left of this gateway to continue following the track opposite as it runs along the top right edge of a field, still just below the escarpment. In 400 yards, at the next junction, follow the track opposite towards **Heddington**. At the next junction in some 600 yards, keep ahead – the track soon passes a property on the left – and continue for 500 yards along to **Church Farm**, with **Heddington church** on the left. Turn left and walk down between a barn and the farmhouse to return to **Church Road**.

Places of interest nearby

Devizes is a small market town a few miles from Heddington, probably best known for the Kennet & Avon Canal's Caen Hill flight of 29 locks, which rise 237 feet in 2½ miles. Or maybe for its beer because it has one of the best breweries in the country, or even because it is such a good name for limericks! The town can boast the **Wiltshire Heritage Museum** in Long Street (☎ 01380 727369) as well as the **Kennet & Avon Canal Museum** at the town's wharf (☎ 01380 721279).

The **Atwell-Wilson Motor Museum** in nearby Calne takes you back to an era that's miles away from today's mode of transport to when Model T Fords, old Rileys and Austins had real character. See Walk 5 for details.

The Red Lion

I t is not for nothing that the Avebury area has been designated a 'World Heritage Site'. That this is important countryside for the archaeologist is clear from the fact that, over the years, three of the monuments on this walk have received a mention in the *Guinness Book of Records*. The earthworks and stone circles at Avebury are 'Britain's largest megalithic prehistoric monument', Silbury Hill is renowned for being the 'largest artificial mound in Europe' and West Kennett Long Barrow is 'England's longest barrow containing a megalithic chamber'. Combine these ancient landmarks with a gentle stroll across the fringes of the North Wessex Downs – with fine views at every turn – and you have all the ingredients that make up a perfect walk.

Distance – 3½ miles.

OS Explorer 157 Marlborough and Savernake Forest. GR 100696.

Fieldpaths, tracks and quiet lanes, with no real hills along the way.

Starting point The main visitors' car park in Avebury.

How to get there Avebury lies on the A4361 – a mile north-east of the A4 at Beckhampton – on the Swindon road. Park in the signposted visitors' car park (fee payable).

THE PUB

The **Red Lion**, actually situated inside the ancient stone circle, is a very old pub, with a thatched roof and a plethora of beams and nooks and crannies. Most of the memorabilia around the Red Lion relates to the stone circle. In the Keiller Room – Alexander Keiller was the man who excavated and restored much of the monument – there is the old village well, which is circa 1600. It is 86 feet deep and is believed to be the last resting-place of at least one unfortunate villager. It has been glassed over and is now used as a table. The Red Lion offers standard pub fare such as baguettes or sausage & mash, as well as fine real ales that include Wadworth 6X brewed in nearby Devizes.

The Red Lion is open and offers food 'all day and every day'.
☎ *01672 539266*

1 Leave the car park, turn right along the A4361 and, in 25 yards, pass through a handgate opposite to follow a footpath signposted to **West Kennett**. Cross an enclosure to a handgate opposite,

before following an enclosed path for 500 yards alongside the **River Kennet** to reach a handgate by a footbridge. Do not cross the river – instead pass through a handgate ahead and continue along the riverside path for 40 yards to a stile on the left. Cross this stile, turn right to a second stile and continue following the river for 100 yards to a handgate and field. Follow the right-edge of this field through to a gate and the A4.

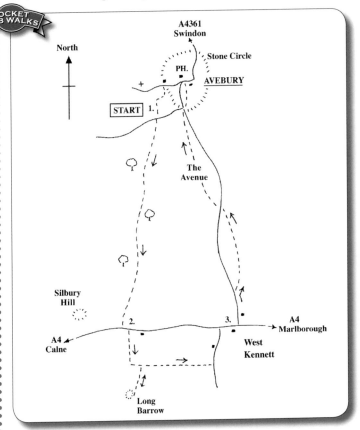

Wiltshire

Some of the impressive stones at Avebury.

2 Cross the A4, turn left and, at the end of a layby, pass through a handgate on the right and follow a signed fieldpath towards **West Kennett Long Barrow**. On the far side of the field, cross the **Kennet** and keep ahead for 20 yards to a kissing gate. Keep on the path as it bears left and continue ahead into an arable field – detouring along the path on the right to the hilltop to visit the long barrow itself. Walk ahead along the bottom left-hand edge of a hillside field to reach a gate in its far corner, before continuing along a track to a lane in **West Kennett**. Turn left, cross the river and walk through to the A4.

3 Turn right and, in 150 yards, left along the unmarked B4003 leading to **Avebury**. In 150 yards, cross a stile on the right, turn left and follow a fieldpath that runs parallel to the road. Towards the far side of this field, cross a stile on the left and cross the road to a handgate opposite. Enter a field, turn right and follow the right edge of this field along to a pair of handgates and the **Avenue**. Walk the whole length of this and, at its far end in **Avebury**, pass through a handgate, cross the road and pass through a handgate opposite by a beech clump. Turn left, and walk the length of a field containing a section of **Avebury's stone circle** to a handgate and the **Red Lion** pub. Turn left, walk down **Avebury's High Street** and, in 100 yards, turn left along an enclosed path back to the car park.

Places of interest nearby

Calne, 5 miles west of Avebury on the A4, can boast the **Atwell-Wilson Motor Museum**. The museum's collection began in 1962 and all vehicles were put under one roof in 1981 when the first hall was erected. The main hall was built in 1989 to cater for an expanding collection of exhibits. A Charitable Trust was formed in 1997, which enabled the museum to obtain a grant from the Heritage Lottery Fund to erect an extension to the existing halls. The 'New' Museum now has a collection of over 125 cars, motorcycles and bicycles, plus extensive automobilia.
☎ *01249 813119 for further information; website: www. atwellwilson.org.uk*

Marlborough, with its wide main street, lies a few miles east of Avebury. An old coaching stop on the London to Bath and Bristol route, the town boasts many old inns as well as Georgian and Tudor buildings. The market is held in the main street on Wednesdays and Saturdays, an attraction that could be combined with visits to St Peter's and St Mary's churches as well as the nationally renowned Polly Tea Rooms.
Telephone the Tourist Information Centre on ☎ 01672 513989 for more details about the town.

The Blue Boar

Ask any visitor to these shores to describe their perfect English village, and the ingredients would undoubtedly include a green, overlooked by picturesque cottages, a fine old inn and the parish church. Aldbourne, the best-known of Wiltshire's downland villages, has all of these and more besides. With a village cross, a duckpond and a 16th-century court house, it is not surprising to discover that much has been written about this archetypal English settlement, including an excellent historical portrait by Ida Gandy entitled *The Heart of a Village*. Aldbourne is surrounded on all sides by magnificent chalk downland, which forms the focus of this walk. This is a

Distance – 8 miles.

OS Explorer 157 Marlborough and Savernake Forest. GR 265757.

Well-defined tracks that cross the tops of exposed chalk downland.

Starting point The Square in Aldbourne.

How to get there *Aldbourne lies on the B4192 midway between Swindon and Hungerford. In the centre of the village, turn off of the main road and park in the Square by the village pond.*

landscape of ancient settlement, as is evident from such features as The Giant's Grave and Four Barrows, which lie along the way. Altogether, a classic downland excursion.

THE PUB Naturally, a typical country village also has a traditional pub and Aldbourne is no exception. The **Blue Boar**, which is believed to date back to the 14th century, is set in an idyllic spot overlooking the village green and is an ideal place to sit and watch village life go by. The interior is just as you would expect a country pub to be, with low-beamed ceilings, lots of horse brasses and some vintage farming implements scattered around the walls. There is a varied menu, ranging from snacks to large meals – including a roast on Sunday. A good selection of real ales and wine is also available.

Opening times: 10.30 am to 3 pm and 6 pm to 11 pm on Monday to Saturday; 11.30 am to 3.30 pm and 7 pm to 10.30pm on Sundays.
☎ *01672 540237*

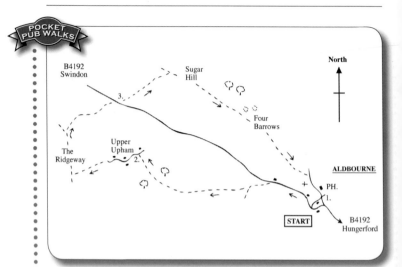

1 Return to the B4192 in **Aldbourne**, turn right and follow the pavement and then a grass verge alongside this road in the **Swindon** direction for ¾ mile to a barn on the right. Just past this barn, turn left off of the road onto a signposted byway. In 150 yards, keep right at a fork along the byway signposted to **Upper Upham**. Follow the obvious track for 1¼ miles until, 200 yards beyond a hilltop spinney, the track reaches a gateway and an open field. Cross to the gateway opposite, before continuing along a wide grassy ride to join a lane in front of **Upham Court**.

2 Turn left and follow this lane through the scattered hamlet of **Upper Upham** for 600 yards to **Upham Farm**, ignoring all side turns along the way. Beyond the farm buildings, continue along a concrete farm road as far as a barn, before continuing along an unmetalled byway for ½ mile to a right turn on the far side of the valley, signposted the 'Ridgeway Byway'. Turn right and follow the **Ridgeway** for 600 yards to a junction, before forking right along a track signposted as the 'Ridgeway

Route for Vehicles'. Follow this track for just over 1 mile down to the B4192.

3 Cross the B4192 and follow the byway opposite towards **Peaks Downs**. Keep on this byway for just under ½ mile to a gateway on the top of **Sugar Hill**. Continue along the track beyond this gate across the hilltop for 150 yards, before turning right along a bridleway that runs alongside a belt of trees. Follow this well-defined bridleway across an open hilltop for 1 mile as far as **Four**

Aldbourne village.

Wiltshire

Barrows. Pass through the handgate in the corner of the field beyond the last round barrow, before continuing along an enclosed track that eventually drops downhill to join a lane in **Aldbourne** in 1¼ miles. Follow this lane to the right, past the church, the **Blue Boar** and the village green, back down to the **Square**.

The old forge in Aldbourne

Places of interest nearby

Marlborough lies a few miles south-west of Aldbourne. See the Avebury and Wilton walks for further details on this attractive market town.

Deep inside the beautiful Kennet Valley and near to the border with Berkshire is the large village of **Ramsbury,** which during the 15th century had the appearance of a small town with its markets, fairs and many tradesmen. Its oldest buildings are to the south of the Ramsbury/ Marlborough road and mainly date to the 17th century. A chapel of ease dedicated to St Michael was constructed in 1856, and the church of the Holy Cross at Ramsbury is an early foundation, with a 13th-century chancel and much 14th-century work, including the tower.

7 Bradford-on-Avon

The Canal Tavern

Bradford-on-Avon was originally a 'broad ford' through the River Avon. The town's wealth was founded upon the woollen trade, with any number of mills being powered by the waters of the Avon. The local cloth manufacturers invested their riches in many fine stone buildings, all lovingly fashioned from mellowed Bath stone. The town quite literally rises in steep tiers of dwellings above the Avon, an unforgettable sight when illuminated by the fading rays of a sunset. To the west of Bradford lies the canalside hamlet of Avoncliff, where a magnificent aqueduct carries the Kennet & Avon Canal across the River Avon. This delightful walk follows the riverbank out to Avoncliff, with the canal towpath forming part of the return journey, along with a stroll through the shady glades of Becky Addy wood. Decidedly a walk for all seasons, but most impressive in the spring when a blanket of flora bedecks the woodland floor.

Distance – 3½ miles.

OS Explorer 156 Chippenham and Bradford-on-Avon GR 825607.

A walk in the Avon Valley, with a short climb uphill out of Avoncliff.

Starting point The station car park in Bradford-on-Avon (a modest fee payable).

How to get there The A363 leaves the A4 just east of Bath for Bradford-on-Avon. Follow this road into the centre of the town, where the railway station is clearly signposted.

THE PUB

The **Canal Tavern**, constructed of local freestone, backs onto the Kennet & Avon Canal immediately below Bradford Lock, at the end of the walk. The origins of the pub are rooted firmly in the waterway with some of its earliest licensees – the Edmunds Family – also being boat builders on the adjoining Lower Wharf. There are two adjoining bars at the front, a dining room and an attractive courtyard, with canal memorabilia being a feature throughout. This is a Wadworth hostelry, with 6X and Henry's IPA, as well as seasonal brews, always being available. The food includes everything from sandwiches and rolls through to steak and fish dishes with all the trimmings.

Opening times: 10.30 am to 3 pm and 6 pm to 11 pm.
☎ *01225 865232*

1 Walk to the far end of the car park and follow the footpath that bears left under a railway bridge by the **River Avon**. Continue across a grassy recreation area to a tarmac path by the packhorse

bridge, and follow this path ahead away from **Bradford**, the river on the right. In ½ mile, where the tarmac path bears left up to the canal, veer right at a junction onto a path that continues to border the river. Follow this path through to a gate, before following a riverside path for ¾ mile across five fields to reach **Avoncliff**. At the far end of the final field, climb some steps on the left up to the canal towpath.

2 Turn right and follow the towpath into **Avoncliff**. Just before the aqueduct, follow a road on the right down towards the **Cross Guns** and, just before the inn, turn left to continue following the road underneath the canal. Once under **Avoncliff Aqueduct**, climb some steps on the left up to a lane and turn left up past

Avoncliffe Aqueduct.

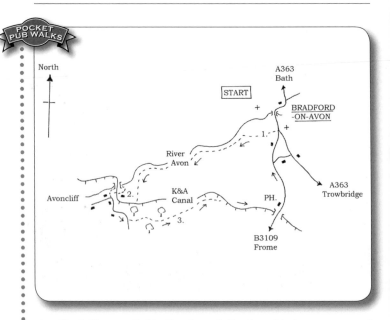

POCKET PUB WALKS

North

A363
Bath

START

BRADFORD
-ON-AVON

1.

River
Avon

Avoncliff

2.

K&A
Canal

PH.

3.

A363
Trowbridge

B3109
Frome

the **Mad Hatter Café**. Continue following this lane up out of Avoncliff for 300 yards until, on a right-hand bend, a footpath is signposted into an area of woodland. Follow the woodland path ahead that drops gently downhill – ignoring a path that forks right uphill – and continue through **Becky Addy Woods** for 500 yards to a handgate and hillside field.

3 Walk diagonally across this field to a handgate in the bottom left-hand corner, just above the canal, before following the left edge of the next field to a handgate in its corner. Beyond this gate, cross a sluice and follow a path alongside the canal for 250 yards to a footbridge. Having crossed the canal at this point, follow the towpath to the right for ¾ mile to the **Canal Tavern** and the B3109 Frome road. Turn left along this main road and, in 300 yards, a left turn will bring you back into the station car park.

The town bridge, Bradford-on-Avon.

Places of interest nearby

There are a number of National Trust properties in the Bradford-on-Avon area. These include **Westwood Manor**, **The Courts** at Holt and **Great Chalfield Manor**.
Telephone the Trust on ☎ 0870 458 4000 for information on opening times.

At **Farleigh Hungerford**, on the border of Somerset and Wiltshire, stand the extensive remains of Sir Thomas Hungerford's 14th-century castle, now an English Heritage property consisting mainly of the inner bailey, and his son's later additions to the outer bailey.
☎ *01225 754026 for details.*

The Duke

The tracks and fieldpaths of this route embrace some of the most attractive downland in Southern England, together with Wiltshire's oldest white horse, an Iron Age hillfort and a selection of most impressive views. The Westbury White Horse was originally a 'squat ungainly creature with a reptilian tail' that was cut to commemorate Alfred's battle at Ethandun. It was remodelled in 1778 by a Mr George Gee who, for his efforts, was labelled an 'ignorant destroyer'. One cannot help but wonder if the name G Gee had made him overly sensitive about horses! Bratton Camp, with its double bank and ditch covering a site of some 25 acres, commands fine views across the

Distance – 4 miles.

OS Explorer 143 Warminster and Trowbridge. GR 915524.

An ascent onto open exposed downland.

Starting point The Duke at Bratton.

How to get there Bratton lies 3 miles east of Westbury on the B3098 road. Park on the roadside – or on one of the side roads – in the vicinity of the Duke, which lies in the centre of the village.

Wiltshire landscape and beyond. A topograph on the summit points out the various landmarks that can be seen ranging from the Marlborough Downs and the Vale of Pewsey around to the Cotswold and Mendip Hills. A bracing upland walk for which a clear fine day is almost obligatory.

THE PUB The **Duke**, named after the Duke of Wellington, has won a number of awards over the years, including 'Sunday Roast Pub of the Year' and 'Best Pub Loos'. This fine hostelry manages to balance the needs of the locals with those of visitors by having a lively public bar and a cosy lounge bar and restaurant. Customers can also enjoy the excellent home-cooked fare and their pint of Moles Best in the Duke's extensive beer garden. Those Sunday roasts, incidentally, are available every day of the week!

Opening times: 11.30 am to 3 pm and 7 pm to 11 pm on Monday to Saturday; 12 noon to 3 pm and 7 pm to 10.30 pm on Sundays.
☎ *01380 830242*

1 Walk back in the direction of **Westbury** for 250 yards to a minor crossroads – **Courts Lane** on the right. At this point, turn left along the unmarked lane leading past **Turnpike Cottage**. In 200 yards, at another minor crossroads, turn right along an access lane to a number of properties. In 100 yards, where the metalled lane ends at the entrance to a property called **Portway**, keep ahead along an enclosed track for 300 yards to reach the lane coming up from **Bratton** to **Bratton Camp**. Turn left and follow the lane uphill for 600 yards to a gate and stile on the right, 150 yards beyond a bridleway sign on the right. Beyond this stile, bear right onto the upper rampart of **Bratton Camp**. Follow this rampart out to the edge of the hilltop, before bearing left to follow the north-facing rampart, with fine views opening up across West Wiltshire. In 300 yards, where the rampart bears left, drop down onto a path that runs immediately above the **Westbury White Horse**. Follow this path along the edge of the escarpment to a handgate.

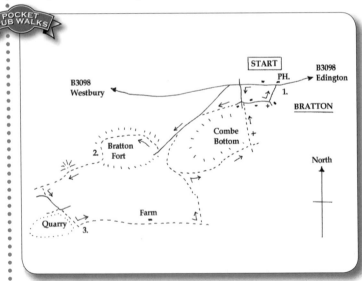

The Westbury White Horse.

2 Beyond this handgate, climb some steps and turn right to walk across the hilltop, past some seats, to reach a topograph. Beyond the topograph and one last seat, keep on the path as it bears half-left down to a stile in an area of scrubland. Beyond this stile, follow the line of a fence across the edge of the hilltop to a stile in 400 yards. In the next field, continue along the edge of the hilltop to some woodland in 150 yards. At this point, turn left and walk uphill across the field to a stile in the top field boundary. Join the lane coming up from **Westbury** to **Bratton Camp**, turn left and continue uphill for 150 yards to a crossroads by a chalk quarry. Follow the unmetalled track ahead alongside the eastern boundary of the quarry for 250 yards to an army checkpoint.

3 Turn left and follow what is the **Imber Range Path** for 650 yards to reach **White Horse Farm**. Continue along the track for another 400 yards, before passing through a gate on the left to follow an enclosed bridleway. Stay on this track for 250 yards

until it emerges onto some open bumpy ground. Continue along the track – it bears left for a few yards and then right. Walk on – the track becomes a sunken way – for 200 yards to a gateway. Turn right at this point, and follow a fence on the left across the hilltop above **Combe Bottom** for 100 yards to a gate. Beyond this gate, follow the line of the fence – now on the right – for 250 yards until you reach a fence post on the right bearing a marker arrow. At this point, fork left and follow a hillside path that drops downhill towards **Bratton church**. At the bottom of the slope, follow the path between some trees – there are occasional blue marker arrows – to reach a handgate at the end of the field. Continue ahead along a hillside path through scrubland to a junction of paths. Turn left and follow a path downhill past the church. Beyond the church, continue down a stepped path to a footbridge in the valley bottom then on uphill to reach a quiet back lane. Turn right and, in 150 yards, left by the **Oratory of St Giles** into the **Butts**. Walk down to the B3098 and turn right to return to the **Duke**.

Places of interest nearby

Trowbridge, the county town of Wiltshire, lies just to the north of Bratton. A major centre of cloth production during the heyday of the West of England textile trade, the town – to this day – still retains strong industrial and manufacturing links. Located in the middle of the Shires Shopping Centre, **Trowbridge Museum** is housed in one of the former woollen mills. It tells the story of the town and its people, and includes excellent displays on both the local textile trade as well as Ushers Brewery, which operated in the town for many years.

The museum can be contacted on ☎ *01225 751339. Alternatively, visit the website: www.trowbridgemuseum.co.uk*

9 Wilton

The Swan Inn

The small village of Wilton, south-east of Marlborough, consists of a few brick and thatch cottages, a pond, the Swan Inn and little else! In the immediate area, however, are several attractions that bring in large numbers of visitors each year. On a hilltop above the village stands Wilton Windmill, a five-storey brick tower mill dating from 1821, which can claim to be Wiltshire's only complete surviving mill. To the north of the village is the Kennet & Avon Canal and Crofton Pumping Station, whose Cornish beam engines lift water from Wilton Water – the canal's summit reservoir – a height of some 40 feet to the K&A's actual summit level. Wilton Water itself is a birdwatcher's paradise, where common species such as mallard and tufted duck are occasionally seen alongside more unusual wildfowl such as pochard and teal. The canal towpath, the hilltop windmill, the summit reservoir and the pumping station combine to produce an excellent walk that will be of particular interest to industrial archaeologists.

THE PUB

The **Swan Inn**, a brick building dating from around 1900, is a pleasantly unpretentious free house that offers a warm welcome to both locals and visitors alike. The food on offer ranges from sandwiches and jacket potatoes through to substantial fish, chicken and steak dishes, whilst the real ales might typically include Wadworth 6X – a fairly ubiquitous brew in Wiltshire – as well as Hook Norton Best Bitter. On hot summer days, customers can enjoy their pint in the sunny garden alongside the Swan.

Distance – 3½ miles.

OS Explorer 157 Marlborough and Savernake Forest. GR 268615.

A gently undulating landscape, with no significant climbs along the way.

Starting point The roadside in the vicinity of the Swan Inn at Wilton.

How to get there Wilton lies 8 miles south-west of Hungerford, on a minor road that heads north from the A338. Park on the roadside somewhere in the vicinity of the Swan Inn.

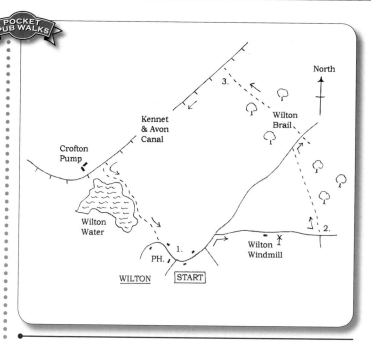

Opening times: 11.30 am to 2.30 pm and 6 pm to 11 pm.
☎ 01672 870274

1 Follow the road that bears left in front of the **Swan Inn**, signposted to **Great Bedwyn**. In 250 yards, ignore the right turn to **Tidcombe** – instead follow the road ahead still waymarked to **Great Bedwyn**. In 125 yards, at the next junction, take the right turn towards **Shalbourne** and the windmill. Follow this lane for ½ mile to the next junction, passing **Wilton Windmill** along the way.

2 Ignoring the right turn to **Marten**, turn left along a track. Follow this track for ½ mile to reach the **Wilton** to **Bedwyn** road. Turn

Wilton windmill.

right and, in 100 yards, left at a gateway to follow a path into **Wilton Brail**. Continue along the main woodland ride ahead to reach the western edge of the woodland in 350 yards. At this point, leave the woodland via a gateway on the right and enter an open field. Follow the left edge of the field ahead down to the bottom left corner and join the towpath of the **K&A Canal** by **lock 63**.

3 Turn left and follow the towpath for ¾ mile to **overbridge 100**, cross a track and continue along the towpath for 250 yards until **Wilton Water** appears on the left-hand side just before **lock 60**. To visit **Crofton Pumping Station**, cross the canal at the lock and follow a stepped path to this industrial monument (www.crofton.ndo.co.uk for details of opening times). For the main walk, turn left by **Wilton Water**, cross a sluice and follow the footpath alongside this reservoir, waymarked to the windmill. At the end of the reservoir, continue along the right edge of the field ahead towards a red brick property. In the corner of the field, turn right down to the lane in **Wilton**. Turn left to return to the **Swan Inn**.

Places of interest nearby

Marlborough, a few miles north-west of Wilton, is a well-known market town on the old coach road from London to Bath and Bristol. The High Street is the widest in England, allowing space for a market that is held twice each week. The town is also home to Marlborough College, one of the country's top public schools. Amongst the many fine buildings that line the High Street is the **Merchant's House**, the aristocratic home of a 17th-century trader. There are five rooms to explore in the house, where visitors can also discover music from the period, costume making and needlework. There is also a library and archive supporting the history of the 17th century as well as the history of Marlborough itself.

The town's Tourist Information Centre can be contacted on ☎ *01672 513989.*

The Angel Inn

Dating to the Saxon period, with evidence of Roman settlement, Heytesbury was named after the Saxon warrior Heghtred. Featuring a Norman church and a recently refurbished stately home – Heytesbury House – Heytesbury was once the major market centre in the area. Today, the settlement enjoys a quiet and relaxed location, fortunately bypassed by the busy A36 trunk road heading down to the South Coast. This energetic walk crosses the fine hilltops to the north of the village, where we also find Scratchbury hillfort. The views from these downland hilltops are immense, taking in the Wylye Valley and Salisbury Plain, Cold Kitchen Hill and the military base of Warminster. By way of contrast, the fieldpaths and lanes in the Wylye Valley beneath the downs provide flat, easy and gentle walking.

Distance – 6 miles.

OS Explorer 143 Warminster and Trowbridge. GR 928426.

Level fieldpaths in the Wylye Valley contrast with steep climbs on the adjoining downs.

Starting point The Angel Inn at Heytesbury.

How to get there Heytesbury lies just off the A36 to the south-east of Warminster. Approaching from the west, turn off the Warminster bypass at the Cotley Hill roundabout. Drive along to the far end of the High Street and park on the roadside in the vicinity of the Angel Inn

THE PUB The welcoming **Angel Inn** is an attractive whitewashed hostelry that fronts onto Heytesbury's main street. Dating from the 16th century, it offers customers a comfortable lounge, open fires on cold days, a dining room and secluded rear courtyard. Anthony Worrell Thompson, the celebrity chef, is one of the Angel's partners, which immediately says a good deal about the constantly changing menu at this increasingly popular inn. The Angel also stocks a range of real ales, which might include both Wadworth and Ringwood brews.

Opening times: 11.30 am to 3 pm and 6.30 pm to 11 pm.
☎ *01985 840330*

1 Walk westwards to the **Cotley Hill** roundabout, and take the second exit, signposted to **Sutton Veny**. In 100 yards, just past a railway bridge, follow a footpath on the right down a bank into a field. Head diagonally across the middle of this field to a gap

in the hedgerow opposite, before following the left edge of the next field to a gate, stile and lane by a red-brick cottage. Follow the lane ahead for 350 yards to a minor crossroads, ignoring one left turn along the way. Follow the track opposite – a waymarked footpath – for 400 yards to a junction, with **Norton Bavant church** away on the left-hand side.

2 At the junction, pass through the gateway opposite into a field, and follow a faint track to the left that crosses a drainage ditch before entering the adjoining field. Turn right, walk along the top edge of the field and, 25 yards from the corner, pass through a gap on the right into the neighbouring field. Turn left and follow the left edge of the field for 350 yards to a barn and bungalow. Cross the drive by the bungalow to a stile opposite and walk across the field ahead – subdivided into paddocks – crossing stiles along the way, to join **Watery Lane** at its junction with the B3414. Turn left and follow the lane – it becomes an enclosed path – for 350 yards to a footpath on the right to

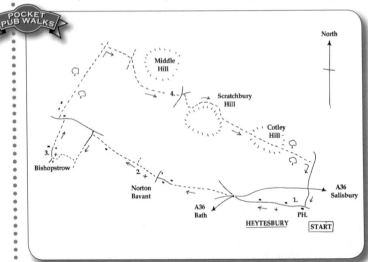

Scratchbury hillfort.

Bishopstrow church. Follow what is an enclosed path, bearing left in 75 yards, to the church itself. Follow the path around the churchyard boundary wall to a handgate and lane outside the church.

3 Ignoring the road on the left, follow the lane ahead between cottages and, beyond the last property, continue along a grassy track up to the B3414 opposite **Old Stones**. Turn left and, in 120 yards, right along the drive to **Home Farm** and **Bishopstrow Court**. Follow what becomes a track for ½ mile to a concrete army road, keeping ahead at one crossroads along the way. Cross this road, enter the field opposite and follow a grassy ride along the right-hand field boundary uphill to a junction in 600 yards below **Battlesbury Hill**. Turn right and follow the left edge of a field – this is the **Imber Range Path** – to steps and a road in the corner of the field below **Middle Hill**. Turn right and, in 20 yards, left through a gap in the bank onto the slopes of the hill. Bear half-right uphill to reach the line of a fence on the hillside in 150 yards. Follow this fence around the southern slopes of **Middle Hill** – a tumulus to the left – until, just past a

spinney in 300 yards, fork right downhill into the adjoining field. Head downhill across this field to a gap at the bottom and a lane below **Scratchbury Hill**.

4 Follow the lane ahead for 20 yards, before turning right at a handgate and following a fence on the right uphill to a handgate and **Scratchbury hillfort**. Turn left and walk along a path that veers to the right away from the fence up towards the lower rampart. Follow the lower edge of this rampart around the north and east of the hillside to reach a handgate on the left in 300 yards. Ignore this handgate – instead continue ahead for 150 yards to the next gate in the fence on the left. Turn left and walk diagonally across a hilltop field to a handgate opposite and **Cotley Hill**. Follow the bumpy hilltop enclosure ahead for 350 yards to a handgate in the far-left corner, then head across an open hilltop towards a tumulus in 250 yards. Pass to the left of this tumulus, before following the path downhill to **Cotley Hill Woods**. Follow a track through the trees, before continuing downhill across an open field to an enclosed track and lane. Turn right and, in 300 yards, cross the A36 and follow the road opposite down to the **Angel Inn** in **Heytesbury**.

Places of interest nearby

Dating from Saxon times, **Warminster** lies beneath the chalk downland of Salisbury Plain and at the head of the Wylye Valley – one of Britain's best-kept secrets – with its attractive villages and historic landscape. The town boasts many historic attractions of its own, including the **Dewey Museum** located inside the library. Here visitors can find exhibits that feature local history and archaeology, including a special geology collection.
Telephone Warminster's Tourist Information Centre on ☎ *01985 218548 to find out more information about the town.*

The Bath Arms

Longleat House and its magnificent 900 acres of landscaped parkland have become one the country's most popular attractions. Several permissive footpaths cross the estate, enabling visitors to enjoy the quieter and more tranquil parts of this much-loved corner of Wiltshire. Starting from the pretty estate village of Horningsham, whose picturesque cottages and houses cling to wooded slopes, this walk climbs to Heaven's Gate, a viewpoint that commands an outlook way beyond the house and grounds towards the Mendip Hills and Central Somerset. Lord Bath himself, the owner of Longleat, has described this viewpoint as being a 'truly beautiful and magical place'. Below Heaven's Gate, there is every opportunity to explore the grounds of the estate, before returning for a welcome drink to the Bath Arms.

Distance – 4 miles.

OS Explorer 143 Warminster and Trowbridge. GR 810416.

The route includes some moderate ups and downs.

Starting point The Bath Arms in Horningsham.

How to get there *Leave the A36 Warminster bypass at the Cley Hill roundabout, and follow the A362 towards Frome. In ½ mile, at the next roundabout, take the left turn signposted to Horningsham. Follow this road for 2½ miles to a junction, turn right and continue for ½ mile into the centre of the village, where there is room for roadside parking on the green opposite the Bath Arms.*

THE PUB The **Bath Arms** is a centuries-old stone building with two traditional bars, a lovely dining room and open fireplaces. It is said to have several ghosts. As well as offering a good range of Young's beers and a wide selection of bar food, the Bath Arms boasts a rather fine restaurant that takes prides in its traditional British dishes.

Opening times: 11 am to 3 pm and 6 pm to 11 pm on Monday to Saturday; 12 noon to 4 pm and 6 pm to 10.30 pm on Sundays.
☎ *01985 844308*

1 With your back to the **Bath Arms**, follow the road ahead signposted to **Salisbury**, **Warminster** and **Longleat**. Continue along this road for just over ½ mile – there is a pavement for much of the route – until you reach **St John's church**. Turn left just before the church into a cul de sac lane and, in 300 yards, at a minor crossroads, go straight ahead. In 150 yards, where the lane bears right, keep ahead along the gated estate road, waymarked as a bridleway. In 100 yards, at a minor crossroads of tracks, follow the track opposite that climbs gently uphill through woodland. Ignoring one right turn along the way, continue for 450 yards to a T-junction. Turn left and continue to a gateway in 150 yards and **Heaven's Gate** a magnificent viewpoint high above the **Longleat Estate**.

2 On entering the viewpoint, look out for an estate road on the right-hand side. Follow this road gently downhill to its junction with another estate road in 500 yards. Turn left and follow this road downhill through the **Longleat Estate** for 1 mile until you reach **Longleat House** on the right. At this point, turn left and follow a straight drive for just over ½ mile to an entrance lodge. Beyond this lodge, follow the road uphill for 250 yards to arrive back at the **Bath Arms** in **Horningsham**.

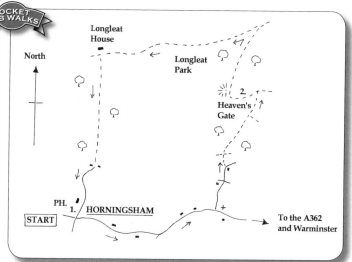

Wiltshire

The view from Heaven's Gate.

Places of interest nearby

There are many attractions in and around the Longleat Estate itself – not least **Longleat House** *(for details, telephone: 01985 844400)* – but if you have time, visit nearby **Frome** as well. A town of enormous charm, Frome has steep, winding streets, a wealth of beautiful old buildings and a friendly, relaxed atmosphere. It has more listed buildings than any other town in Somerset – 357 at the last count – many of them reminders of a rich Wessex industrial history of cloth, agriculture and country market trading. There is a thriving artistic community, with a number of galleries that include the Black Swan and the Enigma Gallery, as well as the Small Picture Gallery and the Artworks. In addition, **Frome Museum** has exhibits and displays that relate to the archaeology and history of the area.

For more details, telephone Frome's Tourist Information Centre on ☎ 01373 467271 or visit their website: www.frometouristinfo.co.uk

12 Stourton

The Spread Eagle Inn

Henry Hoare I, a wealthy London banker, bought the Manor of Stourton in 1718, demolished the old Stourhead House and, in its place, erected the imposing Palladian mansion that is today known as Stourhead House. The adjoining grounds are quite rightly ranked as one of the most famous landscaped gardens in the world. What was once a series of medieval fishponds was transformed in the 18th century into one of the earliest idyllic landscapes in England. Away from the splendours of what is the jewel in the National Trust's crown, the walk follows woodland paths through to Alfred's Tower. The tower is a 160 ft monument that was completed in 1772.

Wiltshire

It supposedly marks the spot where Alfred and his Saxon army confronted the Danes at the battle of Edington in AD 878. It also commemorates the accession of George III in 1760 and the end of the Seven Years War with France in 1763. The woodland is but a part of the former Selwood Forest, which at one time swept in a mighty arc from Bath deep into the heart of Dorset.

The **Spread Eagle Inn**, an attractive red-brick hostelry, enjoys an enviable location alongside Stourhead's fine gardens. The interior is most traditional, with wood panelling and fireplaces, old prints and standard lamps. As well as light food in the pub itself, full meals are also available in the dining room, with local game being emphasised on the menu. Fine beers such as Courage Best and Wadworth 6X are normally available, brews that can be enjoyed in the inn's courtyard on fine days.

Opening times: 11 am to 11 pm on Monday to Saturday; 12 noon to 10.30 pm on Sundays.
☎ *01747 840587*

Distance – 6 miles.

OS Explorer 142 Shepton Mallet and Mendip Hills East. GR 778340.

Fieldpaths and tracks that climb through woodland to Alfred's Tower.

Starting point The Stourhead Estate car park.

How to get there *Stourton and the Stourhead Estate lie just off of the B3092 Mere road, 8 miles south of Frome.*

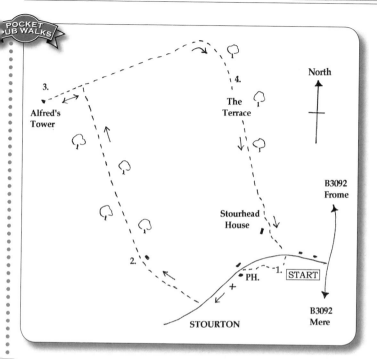

POCKET PUB WALKS

North

3.

Alfred's Tower

4.

The Terrace

B3092 Frome

Stourhead House

2.

1. START

PH.

+

B3092 Mere

STOURTON

1 Walk through the main entrance building for the **Stourhead Estate** at the far side of the car park (no fee payable unless visiting the house and gardens) and follow a zig-zag path downhill into **Stourton village**. Join the road just past the **Spread Eagle Inn**, turn left and walk for 350 yards to the **Rock Arch**. Immediately past this archway, turn right along a path signposted to **Alfred's Tower**. Follow what is initially an unmetalled road for 450 yards to **Beech Cottage**.

2 Having passed **Beech Cottage** on the right, continue along what becomes a grassy track for 100 yards to reach a gateway. Continue ahead to the next gateway and enter an open field, ignoring a track that forks off to the left downhill. Follow the

The magnificent Stourhead estate.

track ahead across the right edge of a field to a gate and enter an area of woodland. Follow the main woodland path ahead – ignoring all side turns – until, in 1 mile, the right of way climbs uphill to reach a gateway and grassy ride known as the **Terrace**. Turn left to reach **Alfred's Tower** in 400 yards.

3 Retrace your steps along the **Terrace** back to where the track followed earlier came up through the woodland. Continue along the ride for 150 yards to a large open field just past some conifers on the right. Follow the left edge of this field for 500 yards to

a handgate, before following the left edge of the next field – **Six Wells Bottom** and **St Peter's Pump** on the right – to reach the corner of the field. Turn right and follow the end field boundary – a belt of trees on the left – to a handgate in the corner of the field.

Stourhead House.

[4] Continue along the **Terrace** for ¾ mile until you reach a handgate, cattle grid and lodge. Beyond the cattle grid, follow the track across a field – an obelisk on the right – to a cattle grid on the far side of the field. Continue along the track – it becomes a metalled drive – as it winds its way to the right in front of **Stourhead House**. Continue down to a castellated entrance gateway and the lane in **Stourton**. The path opposite goes back to the car park, whilst a right turn down the lane will bring you to the **Spread Eagle Inn**.

Places of interest nearby

Longleat House, with its Safari Park, extensive grounds, mazes, coarse fishing and many special events throughout the year including ballooning events, lies a few miles to the north of Stourhead. Longleat is the seat of the 7th Marquess of Bath, the Thynne family having owned the estate since 1540. In 1948 the late Lord Bath opened his house to the public to meet the ever-increasing cost of maintaining and preserving the ancestral home and estate.
☎ *01985 844400.*

The Royal Oak

This walk enables Britain's best-known ancient monument to be viewed from a distance, within its natural setting, far away from the hustle-and-bustle of the tourist traffic. Salisbury Plain is, after all, a landscape of open vistas and expansive views, something that cannot be appreciated from within the narrow confines of the stones themselves. Along the way lie a number of important archaeological sites, including the Old and New King Barrows and the Cursus, a linear enclosure that experts believe could have been the venue for chariot racing. Truly a walk through the pages of ancient history!

THE PUB The **Royal Oak** at Shrewton, with its brick and plaster exterior and attractive hanging baskets, was opened back in 1867. The pub's menu extends from sandwiches, jacket potatoes and salads through to meat and poultry, fish and vegetarian options, whilst real ale enthusiasts will find a number of fine beers available. Wadworth 6X, from nearby Devizes, will perhaps prove an irresistible choice! The inn's sign depicts King Charles II, in that archetypal pose hiding in an oak tree to escape the Roundheads following the Battle of Worcester in 1651.

Open all day with food available from 12 noon to 6 pm.
☎ *01980 620260*

1 Leave the car park via a gate at its far end, join a track and turn right. In a few yards, cross a stile on the left and head across an open field towards a group of barrows on the skyline. Make for

Distance – 4 miles.

OS Explorer 130 Salisbury and Stonehenge. GR 120423.

Fieldpaths and tracks in and around the Stonehenge Estate.

Starting point The public car park at Stonehenge. A fee is charged for parking here, refundable on admission to the monument. If you wish to park for free, there is a wide bridleway just to the west of the car park.

How to get there Stonehenge lies just a mile or so west of Amesbury, at the junction of the A303 with the A344. The Royal Oak is not on the walk, but lies in the village of Shrewton, just a few minutes' drive west from Stonehenge on the A344.

Wiltshire

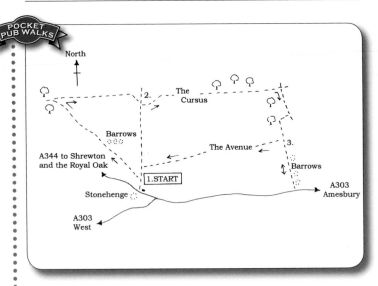

the left-hand end of this group of barrows, before continuing across the open field ahead to a gap in a belt of trees. On reaching this gap, follow the line of a boundary fence to the right, the fieldpath following the line of the **Cursus**. In ¾ mile, on reaching the corner of the field, follow the end field boundary uphill to the right to a stile and a track.

2 Cross to the stile opposite and bear half-left across the next field to a stile in its far-left corner. Beyond this stile, cross a smaller field to a stile in its left corner, before following the left edge of the following field on a fieldpath that shortly borders a belt of coniferous trees. In the far-left corner of the field, cross a stile and continue along a track to reach a crossroads of paths. Turn right to follow a track that runs alongside a belt of beech trees on the right and, 50 yards beyond the end of these trees, turn right along a bridleway to **King Barrows**. Follow this track along to a viewpoint called the **King Barrows Ridge**. At this point, keep on the track as it bears left and continue for

350 yards to a stile and information board on the right.

3 Continue along the track for a further 350 yards to explore the series of tumuli known as the **New King Barrows**, before retracing your steps back down to that stile – it is now on the left-hand side. Cross the stile and go ahead across the middle of the large open field ahead, walking in line with the group of barrows on the distant skyline explored at the outset. Keep on the fieldpath as it drops downhill to a stile in the bottom field boundary. Beyond this stile, walk ahead for 100 yards to an information board about the **Avenue**, then head across to the

On the way to the famous stones.

An ancient track along the way.

far-left corner of the field and a gate alongside the **Stonehenge parking area**. Beyond this gate, turn left along the track back to the parking space.

Places of interest nearby

The **Hawk Conservancy** at Weyhill near Andover is one of the premier bird of prey parks in the United Kingdom. The Hawk Conservancy is actively involved in the conservation of rare species and also, with the new hospital building, does much work in the rehabilitation of injured birds. It is well known for its flying displays, which take place each day during the open season. There are three displays each day at 12 noon, 2 pm and 3.30 pm.
☎ *01264 772252.*

The Forester Inn

Deep in the wooded landscape of South Wiltshire, the romantic 14th-century Old Wardour Castle, stands in a secluded lakeside setting. It was unique in medieval English architecture. Not only was it a secure house, it was also a luxurious residence, with multiple rooms for guests. Old Wardour was intended to impress with its builder's wealth, taste and power. Badly damaged in the English Civil War, it was restored to its owners – the Arundell family – who continued

Wiltshire

to maintain it as a ruin when they built New Wardour Castle nearby in the popular Palladian or Classical style. Having served its time as a private school, New Wardour has now been converted into a series of luxury apartments. Away from these historic masterpieces, this delightful walk explores open hillsides and cool, shady woodland, in a little visited and special corner of Wiltshire.

THE PUB The **Forester Inn**, a traditional stone and thatch hostelry, is a little tucked away off the main road, but the busy car park at the inn testifies to the quality of food and drink available in this free house. What a treat! The Forester offers fine real ales and modern pub food, with dishes such as pan-fried Brixham crab cake with piri-piri dressing, roast saddle of venison with braised red cabbage and sloe gin, and tagliatelle with artichokes and oyster mushrooms giving a flavour of the menu. Warm poached pear with caramelised figs is a typical dessert, whilst wine buffs can choose from over two dozen wines.

Opening times: 11.30 am to 2.30 pm and 6 pm to 10.30 pm on Monday to Saturday; 12 noon to 3 pm and 7 pm to 10.30 pm on Sundays.
☎ *01747 828038*

New Wardour Castle.

1 Walk back up to the 'main' road in **Donhead St Andrew** and turn left along to the **Forester Inn**. Continue for 100 yards to a junction, just past **Mill Lane** on the left, and take the right fork, signposted to **Salisbury**. Continue along this lane for 350 yards to a minor crossroads and follow the cul de sac lane opposite. Walk along what becomes a track for 200 yards to a stile on the left – just before a garden and property on the left – cross this stile and walk

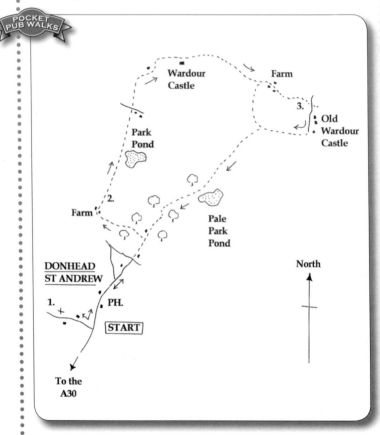

down the right-hand end of a paddock to a gate at the entrance to **Park Copse**. Beyond this gate, follow the main woodland path for 200 yards to a gate and open field above **Park Gate Farm**. Walk down the right-hand side of this field to a stile on the right in 150 yards. Cross this stile, turn left and almost immediately right to follow a waymarked path through the farmyard. Pass through a handgate on the far side of the farmyard and follow an enclosed path – with the farmhouse behind the hedge on the left – to the next handgate.

2 | Enter an open field and follow the right-hand boundary ahead for 600 yards to a pair of stiles in the corner, with **Park Pond** above the embankment on the right. In the next field, walk across to the middle of the end field boundary, pass through a gap in the fence and then head uphill to a stile in the top field boundary to the left of a property. Cross a concrete drive and a stile opposite, before heading uphill in the next field to a stile in the end field boundary at the left-hand end of a belt of trees. Beyond this stile, follow a woodland path to emerge by **Wardour Court**. Pass around to the right of the building, before following a grassy path alongside some rhododendron bushes. Where these bushes end, turn right and follow a path along to the parking area in front of **New Wardour Castle**. At the far side of this imposing building, bear half-left away from the house along a track and, in 50 yards, cross a stile on the right into an open field. Follow the shallow sunken path across this field towards **Ark Farm**. On the far side of the field, cross a stile, join a track and turn left. Continue along this track through the farm buildings and on to a junction with the access road leading to **Old Wardour Castle**.

3 | Turn right and follow the lane that runs below the wall surrounding the ruined castle, with a lake over on the right. Keep on this path as, beyond the castle, it bears right to climb above the southern shore of the lake. In 300 yards, ignore a track going off on the right back to **Ark Farm**, keeping ahead instead along the main track. In 100 yards, keep right at a fork and continue along the

track until it ends at an open field. Cross a stile at this point and follow the right-hand field boundary ahead down to a stile in the bottom corner of the field. Continue along a woodland path – Pale Park Pond on the left – to the next stile, before heading uphill in the field ahead to a gate and stile at the entrance to **Wardour Wood**. Keep ahead to a junction, turn left for a few yards to another junction, then turn right to continue along the woodland path. Continue along this track – ignoring one left fork – for 200 yards to an exit gate from the woodland. Continue along the track ahead for 350 yards, initially passing **Pile Oak Lodge**, to reach the minor crossroads passed at the outset. Follow the lane ahead back downhill into **Donhead St Andrew**, turning left at the next junction to return to the **Forester Inn**.

Places of interest nearby

The 'Shaston' of Thomas Hardy's novels, **Shaftesbury** is one of the oldest and highest towns in England and dominates what Hardy called the 'engirdled and secluded' Blackmore Vale. The beauty of the surrounding Dorset countryside is complemented by the collection of fine historical buildings that make up the centre of Shaftesbury itself. **Gold Hill**, made famous by the Hovis Bread advertisement, with its steep cobbles and picturesque cottages is the epitome of rural charm from a previous time. Located behind the Town Hall at the top of Gold Hill, **Shaftesbury Museum** has much to offer both the visitor and the researcher into local history. It is housed in what was the town's doss house, a place where people would sleep overnight before the great hiring fairs, one in the spring and one in the autumn.

For more information on the town, visit www.shaftesburydorset. com or telephone the Tourist Information Centre on ☎ 01747 853514.

The King John Inn

Tollard Royal was described by Arthur Mee as 'one of the delightful places among the hills and woods where Wiltshire meets Dorset'. It was indeed a royal place in centuries past, for it was here that King John had a hunting lodge. The royal hunting grounds were to be found on Cranborne Chase, the sweeping downlands and hanging woodlands that surround this most delightful of villages. The magnificent King John's House, with its narrow vertical timbering panels of apricot colourwash, sits next to the church. Its restoration can be attributed to General Pitt-Rivers, the father of modern archaeology, whose family took possession of the property in the 18th century. As well as exploring a delightful corner of the Chase, the walk briefly crosses the Dorset border to visit Ashmore, at 700 feet above sea level one of the highest villages in the county. Handsome thatched properties grouped around the village pond create an archetypal English scene.

THE PUB

The **King John Inn**, with extensive creeper covering its red-brick exterior, offers customers a traditional welcome with its beams and open fireplaces. As well as the usual bar meals, there is also a separate restaurant area offering a varied menu of home-cooked food. Real ales from local breweries are also available, typically including Ringwood Best Bitter and Wadworth 6X. Don't be surprised if you happen to see Madonna propping up the bar – the superstar lives on the nearby Ashcombe Estate and the King John is her local hostelry!

Opening times: 11 am to 3 pm and 6 pm to 11 pm on Monday to Saturday; 12 noon to 10.30 pm on Sundays.
☎ *01725 516207*

1 Immediately to the north of the pond, a track heads off in an easterly direction towards a number of properties. Walk along this track for

Distance – 6 miles.

OS Explorer 118 Shaftesbury and Cranborne Chase. GR 944178.

Tracks, fieldpaths and lanes that cross Cranborne Chase with its moderate – rather than severe – hillsides.

Starting point The parking area by the village pond in Tollard Royal.

How to get there *Tollard Royal lies 6 miles south-east of Shaftesbury, on the B3081. The King John Inn lies alongside the main road at the north-west end of the village, but parking is strictly for customers inside the pub! You will find ample space alongside the village pond, 200 yards from the King John Inn.*

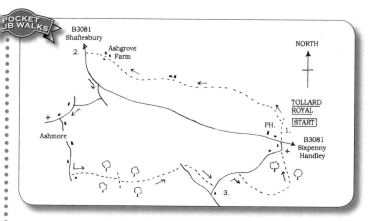

100 yards to a distinct fork, keep left and follow the lower track to a gateway and open field. Take the well-defined track through the valley bottom ahead. In ½ mile the path reaches a gate before dropping downhill to a junction of paths in the valley bottom. Keep directly ahead through **Ashgrove Bottom**, following the path waymarked to **Ashgrove Farm**. In ½ mile, the track passes a complex of buildings – **Lower Ashgrove Farm** – on the right. Continue through the valley bottom for 400 yards to a gate and a sign stating 'road used as a public path'. Turn right at this point and follow a grassy path uphill to a gateway just before **Ashgrove Farm**. Continue along a chalk and flint track and, immediately past the first barn, turn right towards the farmhouse. Keep on the track as it bears left by the house up to the B3081.

2 Follow the main road to the left for 600 yards, before forking right along the side turn signposted to **Tollard Green**. In 200 yards, turn right along the lane to **Ashmore** and, at a junction in 400 yards, turn left – signposted to **Fontmell Magna** – into the centre of **Ashmore**. In 300 yards, at a junction by the village pond, turn left along a no through road. In 600 yards, this lane reaches **Ashmore Farm** – a rather grand residence. Turn left along the bridleway immediately before this property – ignoring a slightly earlier

Wiltshire

footpath – and follow this track for ½ mile to a junction alongside woodland. Turn right and, at another junction in 75 yards, turn left and follow a track gently uphill to reach a road in 350 yards. Cross this road and follow a bridleway opposite to the right. Keep on this bridleway – it runs parallel to the road – for 600 yards until it reaches a lane that runs into **Tollard Royal**.

3 Turn left along this lane and, in 400 yards, look out for a stile and paddocks on the right. Cross the stile and walk across to a gate in the far-left corner of the first paddock. Cross a ride to a stile in the fence opposite, before crossing the next paddock to a stile in the middle of the end field boundary. In the following paddock, cross to a stile opposite just by some woodland. Beyond this stile, follow a track that meanders to the right and left, before passing through a belt of woodland to a gate and open field. Walk diagonally across the middle of the field to the far corner, where a gate and private track lead into woodland. A few yards before this gate, cross a step-stile into the woodland and follow the path ahead for 150 yards to another step-stile. Leave the woodland and take the enclosed path ahead through to a lane. Turn right, passing **Tollard Royal church**, and drop down to a junction with the B3081. Opposite is the parking area alongside the pond.

Places of interest nearby

Created by General Pitt-Rivers in 1880 as pleasure grounds for 'public enlightenment and entertainment', the **Larmer Tree Gardens** south of Tollard Royal are an extraordinary example of Victorian extravagance and vision. They contain a wonderful collection of ornate buildings, majestic trees and intimate arbours, retained in an enchanted timeless atmosphere.
☎ 01725 516228; website: www.larmertreegardens.co/uk
For details of nearby Shaftesbury, see Walk 14.